Life with the Badge

An adult coloring book for the men and women in uniform

Michelle Libby

www.michellelibby.com

www.LifewiththeBadge.com

Happy Trails Publishing

ISBN-13: 9798573351483

Introduction

Welcome to the *Life with the Badge* coloring book. As a police wife, I have followed my husband's career and all of the crazy things that have happened to him. I've written down a lot of what he said and the cynical things his teammates spoke about.

I hope this coloring book tickles your funny bone and gives you a diversion from the grind of the day to day work. Get out your highlighters, colored pens or pencils and color away your stress. Even if you just scribble across the page getting out your aggression, enjoy.

Most of the pictures are hand-drawn and zentangled. Just add your artistic touch and color to the pages. Each page can be taken out of the book and displayed in your home on wheels or in your sticks and bricks house. I hope you enjoy!

If you want to, join me on Happy Trails on Facebook. Share pictures of your coloring and the amazing places you have visited. I also have a few pages that didn't make the book because of subject matter or language on my website under coloring pages. Check it out.

Stay safe out there and watch each other's backs.

Michelle Libby
www.MichelleLibby.com
www.LifewiththeBadge.com
Follow Happy Trails on Facebook

FREE GIFT

Thank you so much for buying **Life with the Badge Coloring Book.** We know there are loads of amazing coloring books out there, but you chose to spend some time with us. That's very special. As my way of saying thank you for buying this book, please enjoy a downloadable PDF Bonus filled with images from some of my coloring books. You can color some of your favorite book covers and other forthcoming coloring books over and over again with FREE printable files.

Please visit www.MichelleLibby.com to download your gift today!

TABLE OF CONTENTS

TEST PAGE

This page is the perfect place to test your materials and colors before you start working on the actual designs.

Red, white and blue lights
are the signs of freedom...

Except when they are
behind you.

I scream. You scream.
The cops come.
It's awkward.

Cop Fidget Spinner

IT'S

GOING TO HAPPEN.

IT'S A MATTER
OF WHEN
IT'S GOING
TO HAPPEN.

It's all fun and games

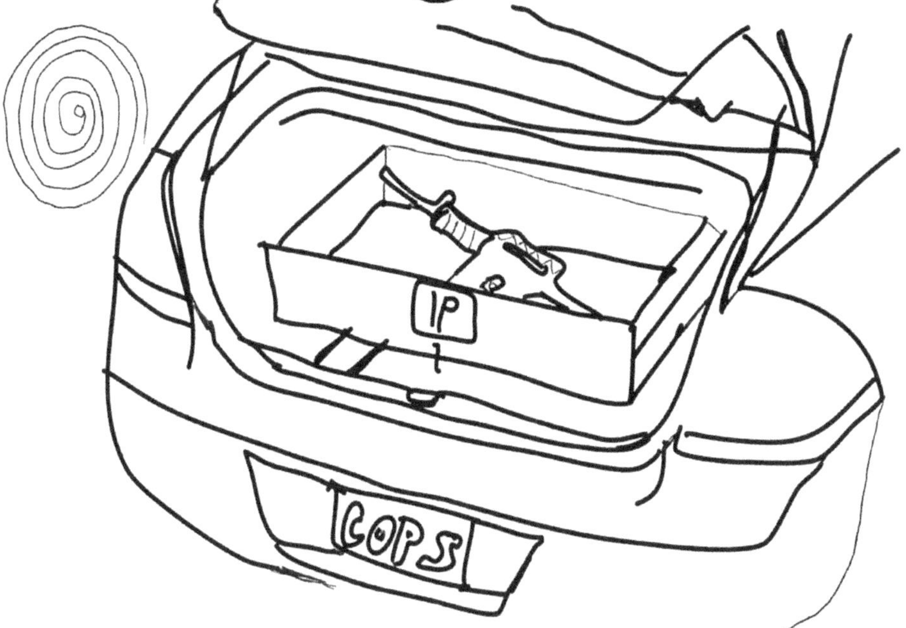

Until they open the trunk.

SERGEANT
POLICE
STATE OF
DIRIGO
MAINE
MAINE
PORTLAND

NO ONE
HATES BAD
COPS MORE
THAN GOOD
COPS.

PD
FORGET
THE CAPE,
I WEAR
{ KEVLAR }

I CAN DO ALL
this through
HIM WHO
gives
ME STRENGTH.
Philippians
4:13

CAN WE GET
FOR SWAT
FOR ADMIN
FOR NIGHT SHIFT
FOR SROs
FOR BOMB SQUAD 
POLICE
ONE OF THESE ???

I only have 

1 BULLET LEFT.

I won't let

them take you

alive.

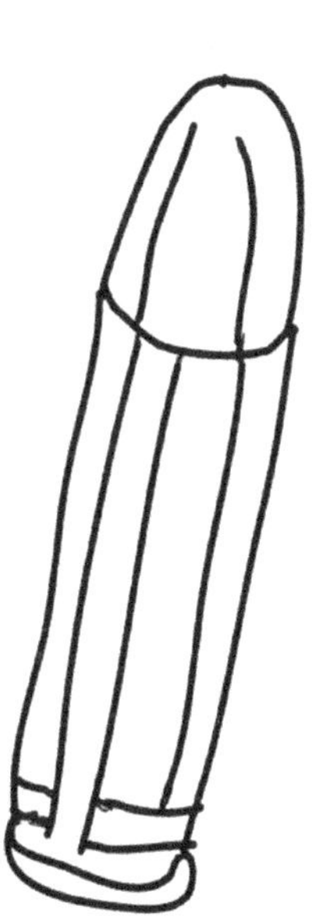

Shit perps say...

"I PAY YOUR SALARY."

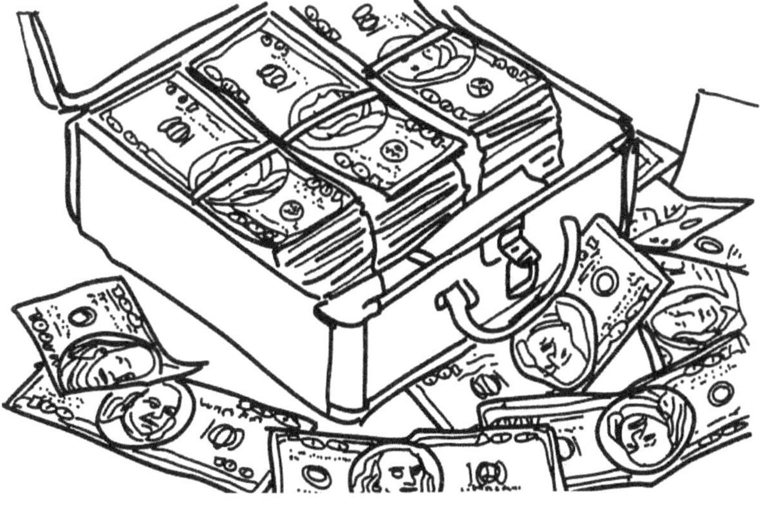

Do
you think
regular
dogs see police
dogs and think...
Oh shit it's
the cops.

Shit perps say...

"I can't
reach my
license
unless
you hold
my
beer."

Being a cop is stressful?

I'm 29 and I feel awesome.

Shit perps say...

"BAD COP... NO DONUT."
$2.50

Breakfast of Champions

I FEED
ON EVIL
OR AT
LEAST
IT PAYS
THE BILLS

Ride 'em rough

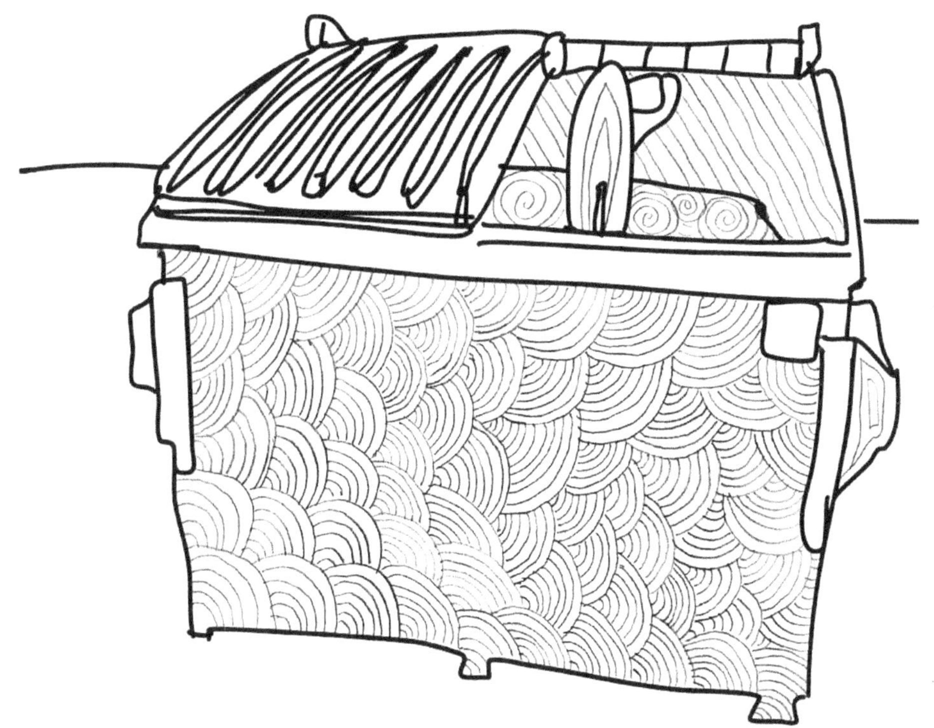

Sometimes work is like
a dumpster fire.

THE LORD HIMSELF GOES BEFORE YOU AND WILL BE WITH YOU; WILL NEVER LEAVE YOU NOR FORSAKE YOU. DO NOT BE AFRAID, NOR BE DISCOURAGED.

DEUTERONOMY 31:8

Shit perps say...
"THESE AREN'T MY PANTS {OR} MY UNDERWEAR."
UNDIES
Wow!

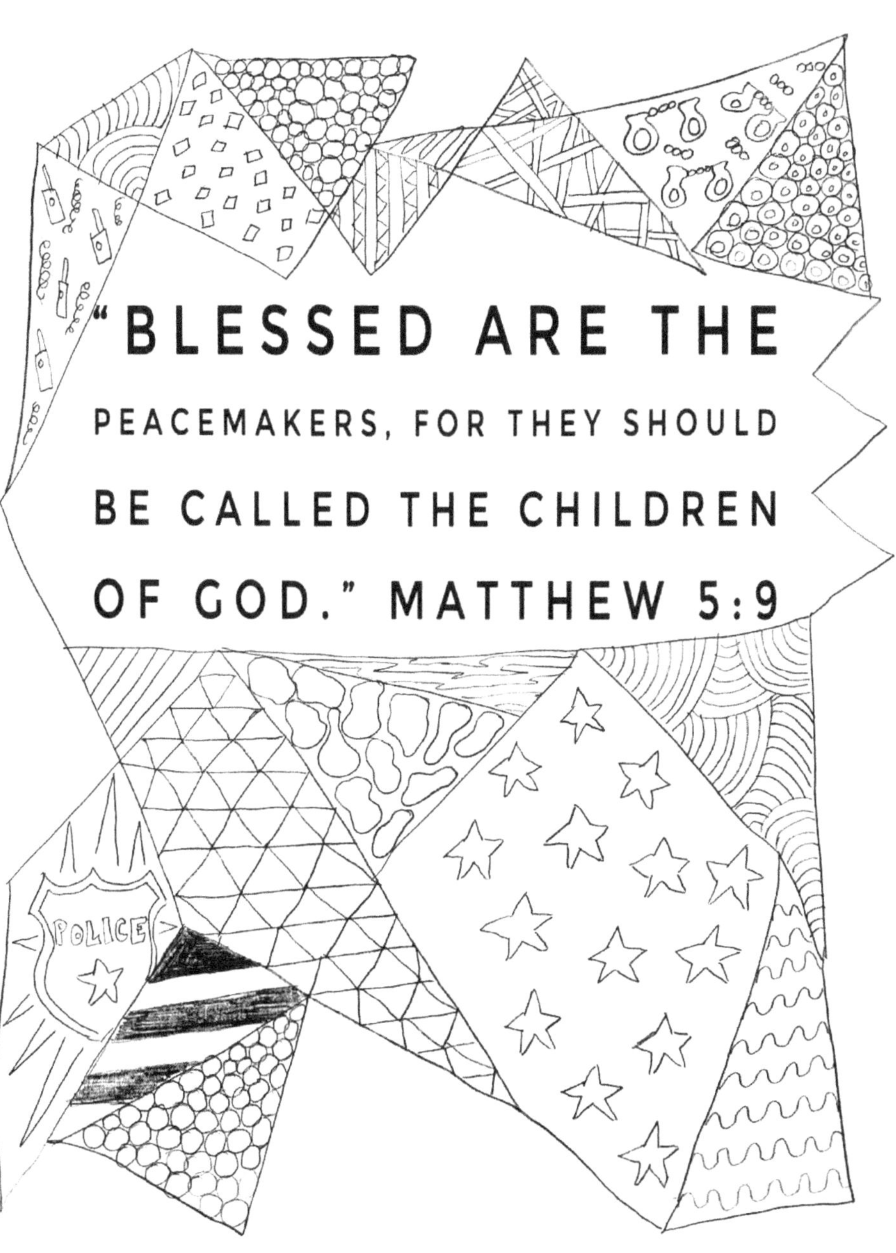
"BLESSED ARE THE PEACEMAKERS, FOR THEY SHOULD BE CALLED THE CHILDREN OF GOD." MATTHEW 5:9
POLICE

SOMETIMES YOU HAVE
TO GET YOUR
FUCKING
HALO DIRTY

Plan of the day:

1. Get home safe.

2. Try not to end up on

I CAN'T FIX STUPID, BUT I CAN

MACE IT, TAZE IT, AND CUT IT.

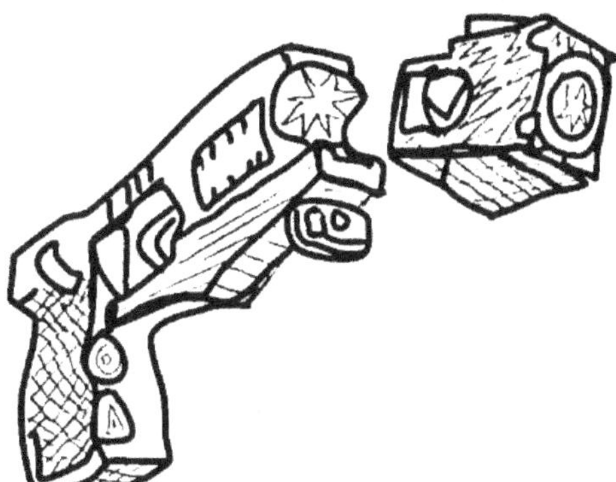

SOMETIMES THERE'S justice, and SOMETIMES there's JUST US.
POLICE

then you will go safely on
your way,
and you will not
hurt your foot.
when you lie down,
you will not be afraid.
as you lie there,
your sleep will be sweet.
proverbs 3:23-24

I'VE GOT YOUR · SIX ·

"BLESSED ARE THE PEACEMAKERS, FOR THEY SHOULD BE CALLED THE CHILDREN OF GOD." MATTHEW 5:9

Life with the Badge

An adult coloring book for the men and women in uniform.

Also by Michelle Libby

<u>Coloring Books</u>
In the Scouting Trenches
Acadia National Park and Mount Desert Island
Travels with God's Word – a coloring book for those who wander

<u>Romance Novels</u>
Kidnapped
Married to the Marine
Midnight Risk
Two if by Sea
Breaking the Story
When the Vow Breaks

ONE LAST THING

Now that you have colored this book, you have the option of leaving a review. I know that your time is valuable, but if you found value in this book, I would appreciate it if you would take a few seconds to visit my Amazon listing and click the FIVE STARS icon.

It might seem like something very little, but every single review counts. Clicking that button shows me that you appreciate the effort that went into putting this book together.

Without stars and reviews, you might never have found this book. Please take just five seconds of your time to support an independent author.

To leave a review visit this book on Amazon.

Thank you so much!

Stay safe out there,
Michelle
www.MichelleLibby.com